Halftone

Colours of desires in absence . . .

Tanmay Chatterjee

BookLeaf Publishing

India | USA | UK

Made with ❤ on the BookLeaf Publishing Platform
www.bookleafpub.in
www.bookleafpub.com

Dedication

For those who understand that memory is a wound that
recurs as language,
that presence is but a spectral choreography of omission
and persistence,
that to inhabit the liminal is to inherit both the question
and the hush.

This book belongs to you—
or to what remains of you in the telling.

Preface

To speak of poetry is to speak of half-truths, of images that are neither whole nor broken, of utterances that suspend themselves between declaration and silence. *Halftone*—a title that suggests the in-between, the liminal, the grainy residue of clarity—becomes, then, both the method and the matter of this collection. These twenty-one poems do not pretend to completion. They stagger, they dissolve, they lean into the unsteady rhythms of recollection and rupture. They are fragments that resist wholeness, voices that echo with the weight of absence.

What does it mean to inhabit the lanes of *Halftone?* It is to walk through corridors of uneasy light, where memory and perception distort into an unstable chiaroscuro. The first five lanes alone articulate this: the rain does not merely fall but bleeds, the mirror does not reflect but devours, the figure in motion is neither fully present nor entirely spectral. Here, every utterance is haunted by its own negation, every certainty shadowed by its inverse. The language falters, as if to admit that meaning, like breath, is never wholly retained, only momentarily exhaled before vanishing into the dense air of ambiguity.

Each poem in this collection is a space where language itself is contested—where syntax fractures, where meaning wavers between the declarative and the elusive. The voice of *Halftone* is a voice that quivers under the weight of its own uncertainty, that speaks in rhythms jagged with hesitation, in cadences steeped in irresolution. It is a voice that recognizes the instability of all utterance, of all identity, of all recollection. A voice that asks: *What remains when the image fades, when the word dissolves, when the body forgets itself?*

These poems are not waypoints on a singular journey, but echoes of multiple crossings—of departures and arrivals that never quite complete themselves. They navigate landscapes both external and internal, tracing the contours of loss, the residues of time, the shifting textures of presence and erasure. They do not seek to console, nor do they seek to clarify. Instead, they offer the reader the weight of language itself—the way it presses, resists, fractures, and lingers, long after the sound has ceased.

To read *Halftone* is to inhabit this space of trembling articulation, to witness the precarious balance between saying and unsaying, between emergence and oblivion. It is an invitation to listen—not for meaning in its totality, but for the silences that surround it, for the echoes that persist in the wake of articulation.

Acknowledgements

A book is never a solitary act, though its solitude often shapes its becoming. *Halftone* is, at once, an articulation of absences and a ledger of presences—voices that wove themselves into the fractures of these verses, silences that stood witness to their emergence. It is only fitting, then, to begin in gratitude for those who, knowingly or otherwise, lent their shadows to these pages.

To the hands unseen yet felt—mentors, interlocutors, skeptics—who, by way of question or dissent, anchored my excesses and forced the hesitations to matter. Their refusals, as much as their affirmations, sharpened the contours of what might otherwise have unraveled in mere impulse. To those who have dwelled in the unnamed spaces of these lines, who have lived, suffered, and perished within the metaphors before they became words —I owe more than mere recognition, though recognition is all I can offer.

To the scholars and poets whose works, whether centuries old or freshly inked, have unsettled my certainties and tempered my indulgences—this book converses, however inadequately, with your echoes. There is no escaping the palimpsest of influence, and in that admission lies the deepest of debts.

To those who weathered the burdens of my distances, my absences in presence, my fractured articulations—your forbearance was the quiet architecture of this endeavour. To the ones who understood, and to the ones who tried even when they did not—both were necessary; both remain irreplaceable.

And to silence itself, which—however unrelenting—taught me to listen in ways language never could.

For all that is left unsaid, and for all that will remain only half-seen, half-heard, half-felt—this is for you.

Lane 01

As the crashed peace of last crops refuses to relent
As the redundant colours steer you through
And the diffident shroud of your breath clouds one rebel
creed
Past the stations of your caution gate
As you write your colours on ground panes
While the air winding through the uneasy lanes
You wade through that steep morning crescent
The transience of the clay drowns the last lost crew
Till some ocean born clouds descend to bleed
As they look to wake again in your southern gait

Clouds, bloody clouds, they rained through the door
That hurls raw nerves to the depressant floor
No magenta clouds. No stopping breath. No cosy clock to
cease!
Never mind! Let these mortal colours fade away at ease.

Lane 02

Again! The lowlines of setting breeze had receded
Into the distance where you thought the limit will lose
And make you cry!
The seasons had come with the rains upsetting the bruise
You once wrote on your wrist as nerves conceded

A little cycle of leafy grey over the cradle of blind wraith
Coasts down the burnt rims of your breath one late
afternoon
Let's walk again!
That smell had you - the last green ascent of the
monsoon
As you moved closer to your wall in reckless mirror of
faith

No dreams had sunk down the drifts of division light
Untouched! Rays in easeless burn melt in darkling daze .
.

Wear your shade!
As you wait in heavy groves for a turn in defeated rage
While the seized day rides past the Iast grey height

The air's so moist today . . you stretch your arm to say . .
.

The words as they break on the shore leaving behind
The you of yesterday!
The restive red beating through the riots in coffee grind
Forces its hue to the casual depression of the fevered day

Sudden stirring in doubts on the pale face of festive coup
Resolves the act in thirsty scenes dreamt last eve
Who was high!
They served you dry as the rest of us turn to believe
The dicey face of closing question picked one by two

Lane 03

A scene collapsed
Wading through the rugged skeletons of his lost gnosis.
An old man from memory passes by the lines of pale
aftertaste;
No excuse could have saved him at this hour of hypnosis
By waters, as the leaf shrunken inside the loaf withers
too late

Oh! frag nicht, wer er war und
Wie er einen friedlichen tod starb!

They were citizens of slow decades
They were beginners of death parade

The mirror creates
An evening as the train left you in crowd of gazes incest
And a rock of grey afterthought breathes by the pores
Of white water that carries the station past the lost
afternoon daze
In a sudden poetaster's sketch as he watches over in
celibate fancy

Und ja! Er hat alles getan, was Sie denken, dass er es
nicht getan hat.

Dieser alte Mann aus Caligrad hat alles getan.

They were listeners of her serenade
They were survivors of bane trades

 As you breathe
 Let me paint a blind kite by the scratches of your sky
 And drown in the heavy steam of your first morning
breath;
 Down the shallow skin of my sleep I keep the name
 With which one could see the films of flying rivers of
falsy

*Sie müssen sich fragen, warum Sie so eng mit ihm
verbunden sind
Sie müssen glauben, dass Sie nicht in seine Erinnerungen
investieren*

They were walkers of ebbing promenade
They were prisoners of the last crusade

Organ of fancy
Flying breathless in psychedelic ease (one cares too less)
Casts a lazy sunset on the moist of your daily lips
And tease the busy anecdotes down the pollens of lunar
fall
As slumber sets at the call of the early evening dog

Buzzing through the buds of a deep lost mourn
Bleeds their bloodless warmth in customary jest

The days end
In desks of dying parlance melting in raging breeze of
hey.
Leaves swim through the dusts of that unfinished
evening
As a story dances in the air at some past hour of pyre.
Failures were the men I sworn by the day I loved you.

A man sweeping his thoughts behind him with broken
senses
Sings of the end course of tide- the unsung homilies of
despair

Lane 04

Yes. He came—
Or was seen in the seeing. A shape, a semblance,
A thing that *was*—or must have been—
Leaning half to presence, half to rumor.

A name was given, or *given away*.
The face, a shade of itself,
The brow thick, yes, but in excess, in accident.
The hair—half-there, half-ash—
A scorched remainder, a memory molting,
A curl curled against the absence of a scalp.

He *moved.* Or—something like motion.
The left foot, the right—disjunct, mistaken,
A stagger mistaken for rhythm, a rhythm mistaken for
intent.
A step—once, then not quite again—
A lurch, a lag, an answer half-formed,
A limb placed where a limb once *was.*

One hand, or what was left of the idea of a hand,
Swung into air, or onto nothing.
The other—*not seen, yet sworn to exist.*
Somewhere, misplaced like all misremembered truths,

Like breath undone, like footprints erased
Before the weight of them settled.

He was—
Or was *willed* so, named in the mouths of those
Who bore witness to something half-lit,
A residue of motion, a body errant,
A presence sustained by the weight of insistence.

Or was he merely the fracture of language,
A thing that quivers between breath and erasure,
A cadence of claim collapsing upon itself—
Each telling undoing the last?

Lane 05

Certain shades in the dark—shuffled, subsumed,
Gloam-born spectres dissembling guise,
A maze of thrums in opiate fume,
Where hunger kneels, the blind arise,
And silence breaks like a crumbled loom—
Crooked tongues in a speechless vice.

Light, a ruptured vein,
Seeps through fractured glass's wound—
A hollow stain,
Mocking the dust, where echoes are hewn
From hands unshaped in a shroud of refrain,
Where the room writhes, unsexed, unbound.

The fulcrum quivers in a pulse offbeat,
A rhythm of steps that never fall,
Yet stamp the dark in a scansion fleet—
Feral, erratic, no pattern at all.
Upward they slither, absurd and fleet,
Looping, unmaking the shadowed hall.

Who was high? The dust or the dream?
Or the ones who knelt in the fevered gyre,
Their tongues unstuck from the gods they schemed,

Mouthing a hymn that scalds like fire?
Hands are lifted, a foot betrayed,
Doubt is the pulse in the pulse expired.

And still they shift—displaced, unsaid,
Their murmurs carve through marrow's pall—
Certain shades in the dark have bled,
Certain shades were never at all.

Lane 06

No! The laurels had asked for a little violence
Of the air, of you, of me, and of her patience.
The skies were wet with
The prophecies we met—

Knew those eyes of the schemes they wrote,
And a thousand other scenes we wished to float.

One too many was played,
A little too close—shot dead.
Yet echoes lingered in the flinching hush,
The hush that bartered breath for dusk.

The earth would not speak, nor would it mourn,
Only the river, sibilant, worn,
Would stitch in murmurs the names it knew,
Syllables drowned in the silted blue.

What song was left but a hollow refrain,
A dirge in the throat of the coming rain?

Lane 07

What happens if the precipice tilts, if the filament frays—
If the echoes uncoil in a vanishing verse,
If the hour gapes wide, swallowing last sighs of wax-
dripped constellations,
If he halts, if he turns, if the dusk disowns—
Yet dawn too is a charlatan dressed in borrowed embers?

What if, in the weft of an unblinking chasm, he lingers,
Spilling himself into the vacuum of unbodied dreams,
Where the waking moon unspools its silk in serrated
whispers,
A hymn, a dirge, a slurred invocation to the god of
second thoughts?
What if, in the hymn, he mistakes loss for longing,
Longing for lineage, and lineage for a spectre breathing
backwards?

If he places his back to the lamp's deceit,
If he unlaces his shadow and lets it bloom in refusal—
What then?
If his petals, unclosed, beckon the moths that devour by
knowing,
Knowing that memory is the architecture of ache—what
then?

If the grey coasts smear blueward, sinking into reds,
If the tide feasts upon breath like a borrowed lung,
If each inhalation is a cipher, half-deciphered—what
then?

And if the question itself is a dusk-lit betrayal,
If the answer, unseen, coils in the marrow of hesitation,
If he waits—
And if he waits—
If waiting is the carcass of flight, suspended mid-
collapse,
A gravity that kneels before no descent—
What happens then?

Lane 08

Speak it. Spit it. Let it slither from the rifted hush—
Whisper-worn, weather-torn, in colors dredged from
rust,
From white that isn't light but the bleached hush of loss,
From black that swallows stars in its ashen, feathered
dust,
From maroon, neither wound nor warmth, but a clot of
dusk.

One voice. Then another. Then a shadow cast aside—
A story stitched beneath, where silk and sinew fray,
A whiff behind a whisper, beyond the splintered tide,
Where words unclasp, unravel, and falter on the way,
Where revenants lilt and stagger—too late to disobey.

It was night. That night. That ink-cloaked aperture
Where silence, choked in smog, made mist of all you
meant,
Where a fair thing once, perhaps, was lost in cindered
blur,
Where memories, malformed, in mirror-broken scent,
Turned fair to fable, turned voice to lament.

Hiss it. Fizz it. Before it stains the midnight blind—

Before the hush devours the last of falling lore.
They are waiting. Always waiting. In the hollow, undefined,
In the black, the white, the maroon—each cipher at the door,
Each hush melting in twilight, each hush never more.

Lane 09

He could spell their names—
A litany of fugitive glyphs suspended
In the haze of must and memory—
Each syllable a rebellious echo
Of an unremembered chant, almost complete
Yet dissolving into the staccato pulse of loss.

Names, unmemorized incantations,
Exhaled with the aroma of forgotten embers,
Spat forth like spectral effluvia
Across the barren mesh of Viesta's twilight,
Where peace had once been a half-remembered walk—
Now a hollow sigh, a cadence unbound.

In that clandestine geometry of recollection,
Where every utterance splits into a thousand shards,
He conjured them, not by rote but by visceral will—
Each name a transient sigil in decay,
A confluence of odour and sound that defies
The linear tyranny of time, yet lurches
Like a half-whispered secret against oblivion.

And in the collapse of structured memory,
The names swirled into an oblique, unruly mosaic—

A dialect of dissonance and spectral concord,
Each utterance dissolving into the relentless void,
Where even the semblance of peace
Is but an ironic testament to the entropy
Of things once held dear, now scattered
Across the disintegrating thresholds of identity.

Lane 10

How distant is the face that mirrors ruin,
A ghost in the glass of recursive collapse?
A thought unspools through the throat of the ruin,
Unravelling silence in sinewed descent.

Once—no, twice—no, thrice undone,
Slipping between the first and the last,
The millionth step eclipses the one,
A foot upon footprints that vanish too fast.

Beginnings are cenotaphs carved into spirals,
Grief in recurrence, a hymn serpent-bent.
A syllable stammers, a cadence goes viral,
Syntax unhinges, the echoes ferment.

He leaves to return, or returns to depart,
An absence inscribed on the door of the start.
He leaves. Leaves remain. Leaves become art,
Veins pressed in pages that bleed and restart.

A mark is a wound where the absence has lingered,
A rupture, a rapture, a whispering seam.
An echo unwinds where the silence has withered,
A script that unspools into fissure and dream.

He is. He was. He fractures. He falters.
A shadow unthreading the breath it bereaves.
Unwritten, rewritten, unformed as it alters,
A cipher erasing—he leaves. He leaves.

Lane 11

The clocks, they stagger—drunken on inertia's guile,
Ticking in whispers where the still ones sneer,
A slur of seconds, bent through the prism of denial,
Where zero and forever collapse to cohere.

A vanishing sliver of boundless expanse,
A cleavage in the tongue of the infinite sprawl,
Where silence is taut as a tightened expanse,
And every abyss still manages to call.

Oh, but the atom—
That blasphemous speck, that sepulcher of thought,
A shroud of cognition in measurable dust,
A cradle of fallacy, a throne left to rot,
An oracle preaching that faith is unjust.

And you—
You with your hunger, your fist clenched in air,
Demanding coherence where cosmos ensues,
As if God should arrange His omniscient stare
To soothe your unrest with celestial ruse.

Hey poet! Say life!
—A syllable shivered, a vowel in drought,

A word in the ribs of a whispering bone,
A requiem scribbled, devoured by doubt,
A storm in the breath of a prayer overthrown.

You wish for the rains to be your rebirth,
To emerge in the weeping of thunder's decree,
But tell me—
Do you even know whence the clouds first gave birth?
And which foreign border will cradle their spree?

Aesthetics grow wild in abandoned remains,
A valley forgotten, a sonnet unsaid,
A portrait dissolving in memory's stains,
An echo, a cinder, a thought left for dead.

So—
Poet! Now think—what remains?
What anthem shall dress the cathedral of void?
Now that you've unraveled the knotted terrains,
Now that the "other" is phantomed, alloyed?

Lane 12

And then the leaves—no, not falling, but folding,
Returning, retreating, unfurling in reverse,
Spines bent inward, veins unthreading
Through the hush of a prayer unspoken.

Southward, you woke, hands laced in silence,
Dew still dark, still waiting, still unbroken,
No wingbeat, no fowl to sever the hush,
Only August—thick with itself,
Clinging to what it cannot name.

And she—she was there, or she entered,
Or she had always been where morning steepens,
Where blues lean heavy against the ribs of time.
You crossed the edges as if the edges were crossing you,
Backward, forward, the cadence mis-stepped,
Feet wavering where shadow had not yet left.

Still dark, still waiting, still unbroken,
Dew hiding what breath cannot hold.
No fowls. No witness. No fracture of wing
To claim that morning ever began.

And so it went. For ages. For a moment.

Until she—no, not arriving, but altering,
Or merely being the pause where change occurs,
Where steep blue hums in the bones of prayer,
Where edges pass, or do not,
Where nothing is lost—
As nothing stays.

Lane 13

What is that thunder that rakes through the marrow,
That shatters the clockwork of shadows decayed,
Spilling its vowels through the riverbed's furrow,
Where silt-laden echoes in silence cascade?

What is that thunder that splinters the night—
Fractured in rivulets, terse in its wane,
A sepulchral cadence in syncope's flight,
A tongue-twisted whisper in ligaments slain?

You come in memories—undone, unmade,
As skeletal branches claw through the mist,
As dusk, dispossessed, by the last supper's blade
Wounds the horizon where absences twist.

That river—ferocious, long dead in its thirst—
Wears in its bones the burden of drought,
But still in its silence, a wound interspersed
Bleeds through the hollows where voices burn out.

Yet thunder keeps coming, keeps breaking the sinew,
As you descend through the wreckage of light,
Folding the moon in your ligatured sinews,
Breaking the dawn with a backward-bent flight.

In regressive nerves, in synaptic collapse,
Where the pulse of the dusk is a hymn never sung,
Thunder still mutters through veined epitaphs—
A dirge in the ribs, an elegy wrung.

Lane 14

All that sounds, all that makes you high
Predictions that you never thought would come true
Come to haunt the dead hedge of your sky
Another day, another time in your words
That breaks the breath of that late evening cover
In hopes that crash the eyelids every day

Yet silence hums beneath the distant moon,
A whispered ache the night won't share,
Shadows move toward some unclear station,
While lost dreams tangle in the air.
The echoes fade, the dawn unwinds,
Still, the heart beats on, still blind.

Lane 15

And then—
The funeral, as if time itself had slipped
Its shadow beneath a blade of stillness,
Was scheduled.

Men stood, chiselled from dusk's delirium,
Their hands syllables of rust,
Their breath black psalms unthreading the air.

At that hour—
When twilight bled through the city's ribcage,
Where darkling flowers swayed like the lips
Of whispering widows,
And crescent clouds, jagged ghosts of leaving light,
Convulsed in the aortic murmur of the sky.

He saw them—
Men bent into the posture of dirges,
Their tools—fractured prayers in the marrow of dusk,
Their murmurs—lacquered in the eulogy of crows.

They were at work—
Unspooling the sinews of the day,
Sculpting absence into earth's mute veins,

Lowering time into the jaw of soil.

O, how the night watched them,
Its vertebrae arching against the weft of loss,
Its breath a requiem, an elegy,
A bruise upon the moon's forgetting skin.

And the grave—
An unblinking eye,
An aperture drinking the muteness of undone names,
A quiet deeper than sleep,
Where the earth swallows time, then exhales it as dust.

Lane 16

Now that you can sign and breathe,
Long-shot days in slow rides down,
One speck at a time on blue ash lawn,

Now that dense surges on those
Clogged veins down weigh you grey,
Remind of scars you wore that day,

The minute of labour is born,
The bronze of breath in mourn,
Its tempered hush unfastened mid-air,
Latticed with echoes of undone prayer,

Where evening clots in copper seams,
Dripping dusk through fractured lines—
A cadence unthreaded, lost between
The pulse of ruin and what redeems.

Your hands, frail scribes of vanished trace,
Recount their language to the dust,
But silence sways, a blade displaced,
Hung in the throat of time, unrushed.

Lane 17

The light, a relic—staled in scent,
A jaundiced breath of withered shade,
Where dust in hieroglyphic descent
Wrote prophecies none dared evade.

It glares, it slants, it scabs, it breaks,
A cataract upon the pane,
A whittled ghost the darkness wakes,
A hush that murmurs blood's refrain.

Behind the glass, your hollowed sight,
Scouring streets where silence sways,
But silence slinks in gauzy blight,
Coiled thick in needle-shadowed haze.

This house is ruin—plaster-thin,
Walls flake like ash from blackened veins,
And time, a serpent stitched in skin,
Hums requiems steeped in morphine stains.

The window shut, the air congealed,
Where daylight bends, but does not pass,
A brittle myth the past revealed,
Etched trembling on the looking glass.

Bitter—bitter, the marrow of dusk,
A venom laced in every breath,
Each heartbeat limp, each whisper husked,
A faithless pact with living death.

Lane 18

And there—some colour—where grey had devoured
itself,
Where syllables fossilized mid-collapse,
Where the mountain—her name—struggled against
erosion's tongue.
A smudge of dusk, an exiled hue,
A flicker of something half-remembered, half-buried—
Or wholly misnamed.

He had given up. Had he given up?
The name had not.
It calcified in lichen-script, in stone-borne murmurs,
A trembling anagram of all that was lost.
Somewhere between a dream and its excavation,
Tropes of color clung like revenants
To the dark of grey—
Refracted bruises, muted remnants,
Scraps of a palette misplaced in the bones of weather.

Had they fallen asleep?
Or had they always been sleeping,
Sealed in the breath of Paethacus—
When first he lifted his gaze to the west's leaden dilation,
To the sky's tarnished eyelid, half-lowered, unblinking—

Where twilight unstitched itself at the seams of ruin?

And then Esthavan—
A name, a season, a wind misfolded—
Came uncoiling down the hills,
His fingers dripping with the hush of drowned syllables.
He did not arrive. He dissolved,
An opaque fantasy rinsing itself through eroded syntax,
Spilling vowels into the crevices of time's indifferent
spine.
What was the name? Who held the claim?
The mountain muttered in glyphs of dissolution,
In echoes unraveling between shadow and stain.
Here, color did not return.
Here, color was a rumor—
A bruise in the mouth of the wind.

Lane 19

Between the brittle husks of speech, where echoes warp
and silence swells,
She flickers—half-formed, unmoored—a tremor in the
lexical wells,
A whisper carved in molten dusk, yet smudged before
the ink congeals,
Unhoused from time, she drifts between the sign that
binds, the void that peels.

She courts the clouds—no gentle waltz, but dissolution's
spectral hush,
A dalliance with absence spun from threads of paradox
and mist,
No lover's hymn in tender air, but forms collapsed in
phantom crush,
Where self unravels, doubled, split—a ghostly trace that
won't exist.

O sky of decaying syllables! You bear the weight of
drifting names,
That wilt before they learn to stay, then spill themselves
within your folds,
A script unwritten, then effaced—where meaning bends
and breaks in flames,

Unraveled glyphs that curl like smoke, dissolving as the
night unfolds.

And we, enmeshed in her veil, bewildered, watching
from below,
Are caught within her mutinous dance, the glint, the
shimmer, then the no—
A dialectic wrenched apart, a wound within the weft of
sight,
Where every presence drips away and leaves us wedded
to the night.

Lane 20

Before you cross the breeze
Before you trust the door,
There come the shades rocking through,
Little flakes of despair.

A hush of hesitant ruin sways,
Latticed in the amber glow of dusk,
Where breath is bartered for silence,
And echoes clasp the hollow musk.

Do not trace the fickle wind,
Nor rest your faith upon the hinge,
For thresholds mock the weary step,
And night distils the shadows' tinge.

Yet still, the frayed horizon calls,
Threadbare with the weight of loss,
Each wavering step a whispered oath,
Each fall a covenant sealed in frost.

Lane 21

I.

No opiate fog, no laudanum haze, yet here I perch—
A cusp, a blade, a fulcrum wound in waiting.
A procrastination rock my throne, my dirge,
And wailstone whispers peeling skin in sating
The ghosts of Ganjshakar's breath—
Or is it his lament's exhaling death?

II.

Dara, oh Shahzada, dismembered yet whole
In historiographic ether—
Inked in Sufi dusk, in a severed scroll,
Or the last gasp of a poet's fever.
Was it the voice of fate that climbed my veins,
Or a mere marionette's strings pulling taut?
The mirror mouthed: No answer remains.
The mirror wept: Your question is naught.

III.

What becomes of breath unmoored?
A drift of frost, a cataract torn
From lips that dream in cadences abhorred,
Cradled by the blue-hinged morn?
What will it wear when it sheds its hue,

When context melts and cadence breaks,
When the hour bends, oblique, askew—
And drowns where the nightgreen marsh awakes?

IV.
Let it climb, then, that blind exhale,
Vaulting gravity's careless grasp,
Curling in myth where the eyeless wail,
Threading through skulls that time unclasp.
Let it dissolve where language cracks,
Where meaning fractures, bends, implodes,
Where history warps and time attacks—
Where the castle erodes, where the marsh corrodes.

V.
And back it drifts, through silvered seams,
A whisper clawing at its source—
No longer word, no longer breath,
No longer bound to any course.
It coils, it writhes, it comes apart,
Recirculated, not reborn—
And if it sings, it sings in tongues,
Unstrung, unraveling, never known.